Fear or Faith, Does GOD Really ORDER our Steps?

Howard Nilsen
with Anne W. Nilsen

ISBN 978-1-0980-4762-7 (paperback)
ISBN 978-1-0980-4763-4 (digital)

Christian Faith Publishing, Inc.
832 Park Avenue
Meadville, PA 16335
www.christianfaithpublishing.com

Printed in the United States of America

Contents

Foreword

About a quarter of a century ago, I sensed I was on the verge of a career change, and I saw that a man in town was giving a seminar on a Biblical approach to the topic, so I went! Dick Sindy chose to use Nehemiah in the Old Testament as his primary model, emphasizing how Nehemiah had, at least, four career roles that didn't perfectly dovetail in the standard way man's wisdom would choose. First, the king's cupbearer; then, the leader of a migrant caravan; then, a construction superintendent combined with military defense commander; then, governor.

Dick's point was—among other things—that God knows how to use our life circumstances both to have us serve Him and others in our current time, as well as to prepare us for something in the future that we may not anticipate ourselves. At that time in my life, I really needed such a message as I was about to change from English teacher to music businessman.

Howard Nilsen uses the context of his own life experiences in a succinct way here to express a similar pattern. I've known Howard since his days of singing in Ted's great choir and joining with us in a care group, and I've heard most of these accounts in bits and pieces over the years. (And of course, he's heard mine!) Now, the progression is congealed into a coherent journey that makes full, encouraging sense to me. Any of us can gain a rich set of edifying messages from the scriptural points and seemingly "coincidental" events he shares, and perhaps, you can hear in his tone the graciously sincere and tersely uplifting affirmation he's so good at and that we all need.

Thank you, Howard!

Timothy Seaman
Pine Wind Music, LLC
Williamsburg, Virginia
www.timothyseaman.com
September 2019

Preface

The writing of this book does not come at a "mountaintop" period in my life. On the contrary, it is during another "hard time." My wife actually suggested that I write this book in the midst of this time of testing and trusting because she believed it would take my eyes off the problems and get my focus on the only real help we can rely on 100 percent of the time—God the Father, Jesus the Son, and the Holy Spirit.

It has been a blessing for me to write, and my prayer is that it will be a blessing and encouragement for you to read. My wife and I are praying that each dear reader finds the time to jot down at least an example or two of God's faithfulness in ordering his or her own series of steps along the "Pilgrim's Progress" we call life on Earth. We'd love to hear from all of you.

If you ever find yourself in doubt or discouraged about the turn your life has taken, think of this. One of my favorite hymns, written in 1897, speaks a message that is still as true today as it was over one hundred years ago. The name of the song is "Count Your Blessings," and singing, reading, or simply listening to its message will strengthen your hearts. The words to the song are:

> When upon life's billows you are tempest tossed,
> When you are discouraged, thinking all is lost,
> Count your many blessings, name them one by one,
> And it will surprise you what the Lord hath done.
> Are you ever burdened with a load of care?
> Does the cross seem heavy you are called to bear?
> Count your many blessings, ev'ry doubt will fly,
> And you will be singing as the days go by.

When you look at others with their lands and gold,
Think that Christ has promised you His wealth
untold;
Count your many blessings, money cannot buy,
Your reward in heaven, nor your home on high.
So amid the conflict, whether great or small,
Do not be discouraged, God is over all,
Count your many blessings, angels will attend,
Help and comfort give you to your journey's end.

Johnson Oatman (1897)

Reflecting on the steps God has already directed in my life is an encouragement to me. Not only is God good, the Lord walks with me AND YOU on this journey!

Acknowledgments

I would like to dedicate this book to all of my Christian friends and especially my Care Group (small group) partners that I have met along the way. Your fellowship and Christ-like love have been a blessing to both Annie and I. You have played a major part in the steps that this book describes.

Introduction

The Bible says, "The steps of a righteous man are ordered of the Lord, and He delights in his way" (Psalm 37:23) It also says, "… there is none good but one, that is, God" (Mark 10:18). Finally, the Bible also says, "But we are all as an unclean thing, and all our righteousnesses are as filthy rags" (Isaiah 64:6 KJV). How, then, can we begin to take steps ordered by the Lord, if we have no hope of being righteous? Before we all get too discouraged, praise God for the gift of Jesus Christ, who clothes us in His own righteousness! When you accepted Jesus Christ as your Savior, you became clothed in a "robe of righteousness" (Isaiah 61:10). God no longer looks on your sinfulness; all He sees is the righteousness of His son, **Jesus**. So let's take that journey walking with Christ!

In practical terms, what does this all really mean? Having been a Christian man for a number of years and knowing some of my faults and weaknesses, I would like to take you on a journey of exploration through my life. Maybe, it will be a small demonstration of what these scriptures are saying to all of us. I pray that as you read, your heart will be encouraged to trust God, **in all** your ways, and to lean not on your own understanding (see Proverbs 3:5).

1

Early Years

In Genesis 41, God told the pharaoh that Egypt was to have seven years of plenty followed by seven years of drought. Egyptians were warned to be wise stewards in the good times to prepare them for the bad, and Joseph was right where God put him to teach the Egyptians how to be good stewards. Although this is an example of God's provision of food, principles of good stewardship can be applied in all areas of our lives. Later on, I will share a story from my own life that is very similar to Joseph's.

Wherever YOU are at, God is not only watching over you; He has a plan for you. He is not finished yet, so trust Him with all your heart in the difficult times and stay focused on Him when you have mountaintop experiences. God is, indeed, very much involved in the steps you take. As you read on, you'll see the evidence for yourself.

Taking First Steps

As a young child, I was taught to memorize the books of the Bible, to memorize scriptures, and to learn Bible stories. We would have competitions each quarter in our Sunday-school classes. We also had something called "Sword Drills" where the teacher would call out random Bible verses. The winner of the Sword Drill was the first child to find the verse in his or her Bible and, then, stand and read it out loud.

The religious leaders of the day recognized that the Bible was a sword (Ephesians 6:17), a MAP, and a tool to guide us to truth. "Thy Word is a lamp unto my feet and a light unto my path" (Psalm 119:105 KJV). They taught me the more familiar I was with my Bible, and what it said, the more I would please God with my life and "my walk of faith." For example, I would be less likely to be deceived by the lures of worldliness or lost in snares of sin and self-harm along the road of life. This "training" went on for years, as my church was my second home, and I went as often as I could. It was where my friends and family were, and I felt good just being there. Does going to church make you feel like you're going home? Do you really enjoy being in God's house, or is it a duty or obligation you feel compelled to fulfill?

My Dad was in the Air Force. This provided a chance to take a unique step forward as a young person. My best friend, who lived next door, was also the son of a serviceman. He invited me to join him in going out to the base to look for a job. The commissary needed people to bag the customers' groceries, but these were unpaid positions (tips only). Because they were unpaid, you did not have to be sixteen to do the work.

This was a very, very large base with thousands of airmen and military kids that could work at the commissary. That made for a very large pool of competitors for jobs. Amazingly, I—as a fourteen-year-old—along with my friend, were both given the opportunity to bag groceries. Being such a large base, on payday, there was a line of people outside the doors, just waiting to get access into the store. With so many shoppers, the baggers felt pressured to be extremely fast. In order to keep this job, I, too, needed to be fast. The fastest baggers worked with the fastest cashiers. This translated into more customers and **more tips**. I worked as a bagger for about a year.

Back to my dad in the air force. Normally, he would have been transferred every three or four years, but for some strange reason, we stayed at one base for about twelve years. Then, when my dad was about to retire, he was transferred to Ramey AFB in Puerto Rico. I struggled. I cried out again and again, "God, I don't understand. I am only fifteen, and I love my church family! Can't I please stay here? PLEASE." But my next steps were going to take me far, far away.

The church we attended in Puerto Rico was very small. In fact, my sister and I were the only two teens in the youth group. Were these steps "ordered of God?" They certainly were not close to my first, second, or even third choice. In fact, this choice didn't make *my* list at all! The first nine months to a year was the worst period in my life (so I thought). In looking back, I see that God worked on an area of my life during that specific time. It was an area over which I didn't have good control—my temper. So it was during this time, and "step," that God did some spiritual "heart" surgery. It was a step I REALLY needed to take, and in Puerto Rico, God helped me take it!

As God changed me, things around me changed. The youth group that started with two teens (my sister and I) began to grow. Another family came with a couple of teens, and they joined our group. Pretty soon, we were joined by another and then another. We developed a tight-knit youth group. We met every Friday night and had a great time in studying God's Word and good, clean fun.

I was the oldest son in my family. In that youth group, God not only gave me the Christian friends I longed for; He gave me two "big brothers" during this time (two single airmen that joined our youth group). They came over to our house all the time just to "hang out."

Remember that job I had at the commissary when I was fourteen? Well, in Puerto Rico, we pretty much stayed on the base twenty-four hours a day, seven days a week. There were very few jobs available, and the commissary was one of them. Shortly after arriving, I applied to work at this commissary. I was told there was a waitlist of over one hundred. With a list that long and turnover very low, my chances appeared bleak to get a job anytime while we were stationed there. However, the sergeant in charge "just happened" to attend the little church where my family and I went. When he found out that I had "experience" as a commissary bagger, I moved to the top of the list, and soon thereafter, I was a bagger. In fact, I was *the fastest bagger* they had.

You see, at this much smaller base, speed was not as critical. However, every payday, I generally was teamed up with the fastest cashier. The step God had me take back home prepared the way for this step. Some of the money from this job allowed me to fly back to the states the next summer and work at a Christian camp for a couple of weeks. This also allowed me to catch up with some of my friends. **God really does care all about our details, big and small.**

I moved back to Massachusetts for my senior year of high school and back to my "big church" family, but it wasn't the same. In Puerto Rico, because I was longing and hurting, I developed deeper, richer relationships with my new youth group. I, now, realized that at my big church back home, many of the relationships were more casual and pretty shallow. Learning the difference about the depth of real friendships was another "step" in my walk toward becoming a mature Christian. Unfortunately, these casual and shallow relationships are far too common in "the church" today. We act like we know so many other Christians, but in reality, we really don't.

When my best friend and next-door neighbor heard we were moving back, he went to his boss and asked him about hiring me. I had my next job before I had even moved home. I worked at this job during my senior year of high school and all through my college years. It certainly is nice when steps are this easy.

Stepping Down the Road

As I shared earlier, my church was my second home. Consequently, whenever anyone asked me what I wanted to be when I grew up, I gave a quick and decisive response; I wanted to go into the ministry. It was the only career I had ever thought about. I was now a senior in high school and needed to make plans for the future. To be a minister, I needed to apply to some seminaries. Otherwise, what was I going to do? Internally, I began to wrestle with my future plan; I wanted to be a minister, but was that what GOD wanted? Was I being a little bullheaded about becoming a minister? I was reminded of Jesus's prayer in the garden to the Father. "Not my will but Thine be done" (Luke 22:42).

This was a major step for me, and since I wasn't sure what God was telling me, I went to my senior pastor. I shared my heart, and he took a moment and, then, responded that if there was something else I could do, I should do it. I was a Pro Merito honor student that loved math. So I applied at the state university which was nearby and got an early acceptance as a math major. On my first day of college, rather than seminary, I didn't think about how God was working on another step in the road map of my life. I was just another excited college kid. I did, however, wonder if I would have time to finish college before Jesus's return. This was the early 70s, and the Billy Graham ministries had come out with movies entitled *A Thief in the Night* and *A Distant Thunder*. The movies made me think Jesus was going to come back before I finished college, so it would be better for me to be a light in the darkness versus being solely surrounded by Christians at seminary.

During that first year at college, I realized that I liked working with numbers but did *not* want to be a math major. So I changed my major to accounting. In accounting, I could work with numbers and learn the rules and regulations in order to manage business operations. In the meantime, I was very actively plugged into my big church.

My youth group raised money and helped send volunteers to work with missionaries in the field. We had car washes, all-night basketball games, and even an eight-hour bike ride one year. Each year, we raised enough money to help send three or four people from our youth group to work with missionaries in the field. One year, I volunteered and was sent along with a friend to Portugal. Portugal had very recently opened its doors to other Protestants, and our denomination had just purchased some property to build a Bible college (later named Mount Hope). My friend and I were the first to arrive to begin the construction work. Sometimes, construction begins with tearing down, and so it was for us. Our first job was to tear down some chicken coops. On several occasions, I walked the property with the lead missionary, and he shared his vision for the property. I suggested that the chapel be initially located in an existing building at the entrance to the property. This would allow the chapel to be one of the first things opened. A couple of years later, that missionary visited my home church and shared about the Bible college and showed pictures of the various buildings. The chapel was located right where I had suggested on our walks of the property. God let me have a little part in this Bible college's history.

Some Small Steps Add Up to One Big Leap

I was ending my senior year of college. The Lord had not returned, and I asked myself again, "What am I going to do?" To be honest, I had wrestled with the decision of not going to seminary for the entire four years of college. Had I made a mistake? Was God ordering my steps? Should I enroll now at a seminary? What should I do?

I prayed, "God, I need help." And once again, I met with my senior pastor. I unloaded my heavy heart about the decisions I had made. I also told him the uncertainty I was feeling about my next step. The gist of his response was that God can use good Christian accountants, and the seminary where he served as a board member was in need of someone. He gave me the contact information, and I quickly sent off my application.

A few weeks later, I got a response: "Thank you, but no thank you." In my heart, I had made myself available, but the door hadn't opened. So I wondered, *What is the next step?*

At the university, they had the Big 10 accounting firms come in to interview graduating accountants. As they came, I signed up for the interviews. After completing my third Big 10 interview, one of my fellow students shared an insight with me. He said, "If you want a chance to be considered at any of these firms, you need to wear a three-piece suit. Without it, it is a waste of time. You won't be considered." I didn't have a suit, so for the first three interviews, I had worn a sport coat, dress slacks, shirt, and tie. This was a little step in the process. Based on his advice, I went out and purchased a three-piece suit for my next interview.

One of the men ("Paul") in the choir that I sang with asked me if I might be interested in working for the Fortune 200 firm he worked for. I said sure and gave him my contact information. A few days later, to my surprise, I was invited to interview with that company. Each year, this Fortune 200 company went around the country and selected ten accounting graduates for a management training program. This program was very competitive, and I got an interview!

The individuals chosen for this management training program spent two months at each of the four group headquarters, along with two months in corporate accounting and two months with the internal audit staff. The corporate leaders designed the program to expose the trainees to the broad scope of the organization. At the end of the year, the trainees would be offered permanent positions. The new three-piece suit I bought was just in time for this interview (isn't God good), and I took a little step in the right direction.

I had been told the interview was an "all-day" event and that I would be meeting with several employees. I was excited and arrived very early, so I sat in the parking lot until a few more people had shown up. *Was this the next step?* I wondered. During the morning, I met with HR and, then, began the interview process. I was quite surprised with the direction of each of the interviews. There were almost no "technical" accounting questions to pass. The questions focused on who I was, where I came from, and where I saw myself going. There were four other candidates in for interviews that day, so I joined them, along with a former training program member, for lunch. After lunch, I went back to HR and was told I could go home. All I could think about was what I did wrong for my interview time to be cut short.

I called my boss at my part-time job and asked if he would like me to work the evening shift. He said yes, so I went home, changed clothes, and went to work for 4:00 p.m. In my mind, I began to rationalize my status. I still had seven of the Big 10 firms to interview with (in my new three-piece suit). About a half hour after my shift started, the phone rang. It was for me. The Fortune 200 firm had tracked me down to offer me, on the spot, one of the ten slots.

It still amazes me how God worked out these steps. What if I hadn't joined the choir because I was busy with work and school? I might not have met with Paul, a fellow bass singer. Or what if I had been rushed and unfriendly, leaving Paul with a bad impression? Or what if I had ignored the unsolicited advice about buying a three-piece suit?

2

Initial Business Career

As I mentioned earlier, the twelve-month training program was meant to lead to an offer of permanent employment. I wanted audit. I was single, and the internal audit group traveled all over the country. It meant seeing the country on the company's dime, so it was an exciting opportunity. Since I had already passed three of the four parts of the CPA exam, this was also the "logical" next step. I believe I was the only one of the ten trainees that had even sat for the exam. I swapped out a two-month assignment at one of the group headquarters for two additional months with the internal audit staff. During my extra time with audit, the assistant CFO from corporate came out on one of my audits to review my work.

As a rookie in the internal audit department, you would spend almost 80 percent of your time on the road with a lot of auditors who liked to drink after work. As a Christian man, however, I rarely drank alcohol. When I did, I only had a glass of wine. My "little light" (Mathew 5:16) was shining, and unfortunately, it made the staff somewhat uncomfortable. They decided not to hire *anyone* from my group. The step I thought was logical and natural to take next was not the one God had in mind for me.

Because I had expressed my interest in working on the audit staff, a couple of other very good opportunities had already been offered to others in the training program. I also did not work at one of the four division headquarters because of the swap I had made earlier for the two extra months with the audit group. With very little time left on this one-year assignment, there were now only two of us left without a permanent job. Where would my next step be? Had I missed out on a good assignment because I wanted the audit job?

But God is good all the time! An accountant that worked at one of the divisional headquarters, the smallest group, announced that he was leaving. So that divisional headquarters needed a replacement. They jumped to offer me the job. Yes, God is good, and I took the next step He showed me. This group's headquarters was close to my parents' house, so I didn't even need to move.

In hindsight, this was probably the best opportunity available to anyone on this program over a five-plus-year period. Part of my job was to review all capital projects and expenditures within this group (approximately ten million dollars a year). Shortly after I arrived, however, corporate, having recently purchased two international oil and gas companies—each with three hundred million dollars a year in sales—decided to assign them to my division. Immediately, this changed us from the smallest division to the largest division. With major spending by corporate focused on oil and gas, my capital budget jumped to two hundred million dollars a year. The capital spending I was responsible for was now a major focal point for the entire company.

I believe God is at work all the time in our lives and is directing our paths, even when we are clueless. Many times, we "miss" a major hurt because our path is slightly altered by, what some would describe as, just a "coincidence." What I am trying to say is that I could cite thousands of examples of steps people took before realizing later that something more than mere coincidence had resulted in an unexpected, God-driven benefit. The ones I am sharing from my own life are what I would classify as clear examples of God's intervention. The total impact of these big and little steps will only be known when I get to heaven.

Time for The Two-Step

My employer recognized high turnover at one of the newly purchased oil subsidiaries. I was asked to relocate to the subsidiary's headquarters in Houston, Texas. I mentioned earlier that I had passed three parts of the CPA exam. In most states, you have three years to complete all four parts of the exam. Then, to obtain the CPA license, you also had to acquire work experience as an auditor. Since I didn't work in auditing, I didn't have the experience needed. Also, my three-year window to pass the fourth part had expired. In Texas, however, it was a five-year window! AND they would consider technical work within industry that was validated by a Texas CPA. Taking this step (the move to Texas) meant I could still pass the fourth part of the CPA exam and get my technical industry experience credited toward the experience requirement of the Texas State Board of Public Accountancy. At that time, the exam was only offered twice a year, so the next time it was offered, I sat for the fourth part and passed. My boss, a Texas CPA, wrote the required letter of recommendation. I was now a certified Texas CPA. This step was critical for several future steps to take place.

Steps Within Steps

Shortly after getting my Texas CPA license, oil prices tanked, and I was stuck in a bad marketplace. It was a terrible time to have to sell a home. Jobs were gone, and interest rates were very high for mortgages. I reached out to the headquarters group I had previously worked at, but they did not have any openings. They did, however, search on my behalf for a place for me to transfer to. The Power Generation Group agreed to create a job for me back home, in Connecticut.

In fact, this job was a promotion! The Texas oil company was an international operation, and I was responsible at their corporate office for domestic and international accounting. At my new job, the group was expanding their international accounting operations, and my Texas experience prepared the way for me to assist with the expansion. God is sooo good. I got a promotion, I got my CPA license, and I got international experience during this one-year assignment to prepare me for the next step.

The company's relocation policy allowed me to sell my home back to the company. Obviously, moving was a big "STEP," and a new job was a big step, but there is another "step" buried in all this travelling.

My new home was just four miles from the office, but a fair distance from the church I grew up attending and loving so dearly. As it turns out, I would have to drive almost directly by a sister church in order to get there. My home church had a big choir (I loved singing in the choir), it had two church softball teams (I loved to play), and it had its own internal men's basketball league. It had lots of programs and things to be involved with. The sister church, however, didn't have any of these things. Its attendance was a little over one hundred. I wrestled with the question of which church to attend. For the third time, I went to inquire of the same senior pastor. I told him the small sister church needed a lot of help. "What should I do?" I asked. He reminded me that although my home church was quite large, it too had great opportunities of service for me to immediately plug into. Although the pastor encouraged me to come home, I was torn. After a little more prayer, I felt certain the next step that GOD was leading me to take was to plug into the local church, even though my home church was within reasonable driving distance.

The Next Step

Having made the decision to attend the smaller sister church, how was I going to serve there? The answer didn't—like in most cases—come immediately. God worked on my heart (and others' hearts as well). My heart ached for a choir, and I knew that the church had some extremely talented and committed people who were far more qualified than me. But in so many situations that I have seen, God calls *servants* with servants' hearts. Then, He can take care of the rest. So I reached out to the pastor about starting a choir. I was amazed at his response. His wife was the church pianist, and the two of them had been talking and praying about a choir and someone to lead it. He was excited. My earlier indecision about which church to attend started to make a lot more sense. God had been orchestrating my steps once again.

We put out an announcement, and seven others signed up. However, a few very talented members did not. Counting me, we had two basses, three altos, and three sopranos. We also had some good microphones. We had no budget, so I wrote a little Christmas story and intertwined a few Christmas songs from the hymnal, sung in three-part harmony.

Little is much in the hands of God, and He blessed our faithfulness. In fact, the Sunday we sang our Christmas program, a few more singers, including a couple of tenors, immediately joined our ranks. One of the tenors, who was also a board member, shared that he didn't sign up earlier because a previous attempt for a choir failed, and he did not have the time to "waste" if it was going to fail again. As a side note, it is safe to say that he was not alone in that feeling. There are *so* many who listen to similar negative thoughts and, then, make excuses when asked to serve. Did you ever consider the real source of such negativity? The truth is that no act of service goes to waste, but the enemy of our souls will always be at hand to drive discouragement. He will happily provide excuses to avoid serving God, if we let him.

A Billy Graham crusade was going to be held in Hartford, a short distance from my home. The ministry reached out to the local churches for people to sing in the choir each night. I love to sing, so I volunteered. I joined approximately one thousand others to sing God's praises. I could sing my heart out, and if I made a mistake, no one would know. I did not have to be a professional—simply someone who loved God and was willing to SERVE. It is amazing how many opportunities there are if you simply open your eyes and agree to be an available servant.

About a year later, another major step was asked of me. That same tenor/board member had a couple of teenagers who were part of the youth group. However, the youth group was dying. The ministry to the teens was ineffective, and this parent was crying out for help. His girls didn't want to go. He volunteered to take over the choir if I would become the youth director. The choir was now an effective ministry in the church, and he was plugged in 100 percent. I accepted his offer and began serving the youth of the church as their youth director. God is good, and He blessed us. The youth group grew, and teens were making serious commitments to the Lord. During this time, I also became the treasurer of the church (another step). But I was about to take a much bigger step. A life-changing step.

3

Full-Time Ministry

The decision I made many years earlier was still tugging at my heart, so I decided to take the Bible courses necessary to get licensed and enter the ministry. These courses encouraged my heart, and in no time, I was done. I was ready. Now, my prayer was, "Lord, I have done my part. If this is really what You want me to do, then, please open a door." Less than a month after I completed the courses, a church on Cape Cod contacted me about an opening on their ministry staff and asked if I would like to interview. I hadn't even put a resume together yet, but I went to the interview and was offered the job. This was a church with a school and a day care. I was to be the youth pastor *and* the business manager, handling the books for all three ministries.

After I was hired, the senior pastor told me that he and his wife knew my parents over thirty years earlier! They had attended the same church. Even so, I believed, then (and I believe now), I wouldn't have gotten the offer had I not gone to the smaller church and become its volunteer treasurer and youth director. Oh, one more steppingstone: the pastor who handled counseling at this church on Cape Cod was the other bass in the eight-person choir that I started a couple of years earlier. He was also aware of me taking the Bible courses. These prior steps—ordered by the Lord—paved the way to my next step. I was now in full-time ministry. And those years as a CPA would assist me greatly.

This new ministry position required another move, so I had a house to sell and a new house to buy. Once again, I prayed, "Lord, I believe you are directing our path, please, help me to sell my home." It was, by no means, a seller's market, but I put out a "For Sale by Owner" sign and had a Saturday open house. Someone came in and looked around. While she was still there, a second party came to look. The first party appeared to be very interested, thanked us for letting her tour, and went on her way. The second party looked and asked a few questions. Before they left, a third party came to look. These were the only people that came to the first open house, but to the "middle" party, it looked like this was a hot property. The following weekend, we had one person come by, just before the "middle party" from the first open house came to make an offer. The offer was a full-price offer! God is good all the time. All the time, God is GOOD.

At my new church home on the cape, I joined its small choir. One day, rather unexpectedly, the senior pastor asked me to sing a solo. I had never sung a solo before, but I was reminded that God looks for *available* servants. I said, "Yes," and selected the song, "Through It All," by Andre Crouch. One of the other pastors, my friend and choir member from the previous church, played the guitar and agreed to accompany me. He was very busy and could not arrange a time for us to practice. Sunday morning, I thought I was ready. I knew the words and the melody. However, my partner was not so ready. Consequently, he repeatedly changed keys at random. As hard as I tried to stay on key, I *failed*. After the first verse, I stopped, apologized, and said, "I'm going to **read** the rest of the words, and I hope the **words** may touch your heart."

Wow, I felt like I had blown it big time! I thought, *I am so sorry, God.* It was my first solo as a singer, and I thought I had failed. Then, God showed me differently. One of the ladies in the church came up to me the next week. She said, "Thank you for singing last week. I have been so afraid of making mistakes that I have not been willing to serve. You, one of the pastors, showed me last week that it's okay if you make mistakes. God is just looking for available servants."

About four to six weeks later, there was a knock on my house door. When I opened my door, there stood a stranger. The woman standing there told me she had been on the way to the hospital to visit a friend, when she was led by God to stop in for a moment at my church. She arrived just when I was "singing." She left immediately after my song was done. She had now come to my home to ask for a copy of the **words** to the song I had been singing. Her friend in the hospital had passed away, and she wanted the words read at the funeral.

There were many times before—and after—the day of my first solo when I was clearly **not** the most qualified person around to perform a service for the Lord. Unlike others, however, I have tried to be an available servant, ready to risk embarrassment or suffer inconvenience in order to take the step God has for me. (What about you? Are you available when God asks you to serve?)

More Building Steps

Sometime later, a small church, not too far away, invited me to come be its assistant pastor. My first assignment was teaching an adult Sunday-school class on stewardship of finances. I was able to take God's Word and my accounting background to develop a course to help young families manage their finances in a manner that would be pleasing to God. The course materials dealt with stewardship as it related to tithes and offerings to God. The second part dealt with management of home finances based on Biblical principles.

Several months later, the deacon board asked me to meet with the minister of music on this very same topic. About two years later, this music minister wrote me a letter thanking me for our meetings. He had wrestled with the idea of pastoring a church because his poor handling of finances at home was holding him back. Our one-on-one training encouraged him to take the next step in his walk with Christ. As a result, he told me he had just accepted a senior pastor position up in Maine.

This small new church that I was now a part of was young, and the leadership didn't have a budget. As a result, they operated from check balance to check balance. They had just begun a new church building program with no one qualified to manage the business side of the process. This new facility was not a two-hundred-million-dollar capital program, but my business steps in earlier years prepared the way for me to manage the building program as chairman and establish the financial reporting needed. A businessman, and now a new dear friend, served with me on the building committee. We developed a relationship which has lasted for many years. He has been involved in many of the steps I went on to take in life, and it began here in helping this little church build a sanctuary.

The church budget was limited, so I needed a second paying job. My CPA background made finding something much easier, and this "second" job became the basis for another step I would take in the future. It brings me peace to know God sure does know what He is doing, even if I am totally unaware at the time. Can you relate?

Well It's Time for Another Step

I decided to interview for a lead pastor position at a very small church in the south. I was a northerner, so the customs, culture, facilities, and leadership style were a little different for me. For example, the congregation met in a block building with two space heaters. It was a far cry from the new church that we had just constructed on Cape Cod. There was a lean-to in the back with dirt floors for two tiny classrooms and NO bathrooms. (You needed to make sure you used the facilities before you came to church.) The church board had bought land across the street and had even put in a foundation for a new church building. Unfortunately, a church split followed by high turnover in the pulpit (two pastors lasted for less than a year) had devastated this ministry.

I suggested the church leaders pray about my candidacy and said I would do the same. I promised to call the board members in a week to discuss the matter further. I was so glad when I got in the car to drive home. This did NOT appear—to my eye—to be a "golden opportunity." Not even close. God has told us in His Word, however, to "lean not on your own understanding" (Proverbs 3:5).

I had agreed with the church leadership to pray, and I did. This was not my first choice, but it probably wasn't very different than what most missionaries encounter in the mission field. I prayed about the possibility of making such a major life-changing commitment. In talking to God, I agreed in my heart to ask directly if these prospective employers had, in fact, prayed about my coming. To my surprise, I was told that every night that week, they opened their church for prayer. My heart melted before God. He sees what we cannot. God had directed the next step.

This step did not come without challenges, however. The real-estate market was soft, but thankfully, we found someone to rent our home on Cape Cod. The church could only pay $133.00 per week, just enough to cover the rent on a small house in town. But what about my car payment, electricity, gas, insurance, telephone, clothes for me and my family, and oh, yeah, can't forget food?

Remember that story of Egypt and the seven years of plenty? Well, God had given us a few years of plenty at that Fortune 200 firm, and now, during the drought, we could tap into the reserve set aside. God had provided, we were reasonable stewards, so His provision was there to meet the needs.

For a lot of Christians, however, this would have been a serious problem. It is, sometimes, very hard to let go of "our possessions." After all, what about being a good steward and setting something aside for retirement or the kid's college or a nice vacation? God knows the future; I don't. That is what a walk of faith is all about; putting our trust in HIM. ALL we have, God has provided.

Prior to the split I mentioned, this little church had purchased some land for the building of a new facility—a real church building. They didn't just buy some land, they purchased one hundred acres—far more than they needed. However, they split the land into two pieces. One piece (thirty-five acres) was for the church, and the second was subdivided for a housing development. They sold lots, and the proceeds were placed in a building fund account. Once again, because of my business background, I put together a capital budget for the church building. We had just about all we needed for the planned facility. So now, I became a carpenter and the pastor as we began the building of the church across the street. Having already assisted a brother-in-law with a few home-improvement projects, I was also familiar with how to wire a building. These steps taught me the skills needed to wire the entire new church, saving us thousands of dollars the church didn't have. In three or four months, we completed the new church facility.

A Step of Provision

Shortly after completing the church building and moving in, my "years of plenty" funds were running dry. I cried out to God for help. What I did not know was that God had already prepared the way for me to take my next step. The pastor's wife in the next town over was the executive secretary to the president of the local college. The president was informed that the sole accounting professor at the college (which offered an accounting major) had suddenly quit. The next semester was about to begin in a couple of weeks. Somehow, his secretary had heard that even though I was a pastor, I also had a masters in accounting and was a CPA. She called me and asked if I had any interest in teaching at the college, as well as continuing on as a pastor. God was supplying our needs! I taught all accounting courses offered on a rotating two-year schedule.

There is another aspect to this time in my life that should be addressed. It has to do with vision (Proverbs 29:18). When I came to this small church, I believed, in my heart, that if I would preach the Word and be the man of God HE wanted me to be, this Church of 28 would be 128 within a year. Otherwise, why would God want my next step to be way down south into such a small little town? Well, as you might have guessed, we didn't hit 128. In fact, our average was 35, and the next year was 45. I wondered, *Had I really taken the right steps?* Were they ordered by the Lord? Why wasn't I making the impact I thought I should, i.e. creating a growing church? When we don't see what we expect, the enemy jumps in to get us to question the steps we are taking.

I believe God spoke to my heart and opened my eyes to see the answer. This was a very small town where it seemed like everyone knew everything about everyone. The eyes of this town were on this fractured church to see what was going to happen. Healing takes time, and sometimes, God calls us to a place where we are the instruments used in this slow healing process. My job was to plant seeds and water, BUT GOD giveth the increase! See 1 Corinthians 3:7. During the next year, God did just that, and I saw the growth I had prayed for!

Different Kind of Steps

The father of one of the new families had been involved in a prison ministry for several years. One day after church, as I was shaking his hand, he asked me if I would like to join him the next time he was going to the prison. I was thrilled to be invited! He was a little shocked I was interested at all. As it turned out, he had previously asked a couple of other pastors to join him, and they had declined. They were "busy" with church stuff, and this wasn't their ministry. I made it a priority to join him and his teams each month. He did the preaching. I was there to support him and to encourage prisoners on a one-on-one basis. In fact, several months later, we had the prison choir come and sing at one of our Sunday-morning services.

Sometimes, we get too hung up on *our* role in a ministry. Jesus saw the two mites the poor widow woman gave and praised her gift. Why? Because God **always** looks at our hearts when we speak or act (see Luke 21:1–4). He sees our love and devotion. He knows when we give with our whole heart, and He blesses us when we do.

A Fellowship Step

The ministers in town met once a month for some fellowship; however, several ministers refused to be a part it because of a few theological differences. And if, by chance, one went to a meeting, they seemed to think it was their responsibility to address these differences. My predecessors were in this group. I believe God desires us to major in the majors and minor in the minors. They were a little surprised and a little guarded when I first joined them. After a few months of simple fellowship and words of encouragement, the walls came down. After all, we were just co-laborers for the kingdom of God.

The second year of my ministry in this town, I was invited to preach at the combined community thanksgiving church service which was held in one of "their" church sanctuaries.

I also play the accordion, and I was invited to every one of these minister's churches to play music and, then, share at their Saturday-morning senior fellowship meetings. God knows how much I love to sing and play worship music. Wasn't it a pure and lovely thing that He matched the desires of my heart with the needs of that little town? (See Philippians 4:8 and Psalm 37:4.)

Not Done Yet

I received a call from a businessman I had worked with while I was the assistant pastor in New England. He asked if I would consider helping him start a new company. He knew I was in the ministry, so he asked if, maybe, I could "transfer" to a church near where this business was starting. I explained to him that I used to live not too far from there, and it did not have a church (never mind it needing a new pastor and being willing to consider me as a candidate when I lived so far away). A week or two later, the denomination's New England district superintendent called me and asked if I would pray about a position as senior pastor at a church (in the same town where my businessman acquaintance was going to open a new business). The superintendent told me that congregation had asked for me specifically!

Apparently, soon after I had moved south, another minister pioneered a new church in the town in question. He was leaving to teach at a seminary which created the need for another pastor to take his place. **Statistically, I think I had a better chance to win the lottery than for this series of events to have "just happened."** As a result, even though I loved the church where I was at, I felt compelled to candidate for the position.

So I went there to preach as part of my candidacy. During my meeting with the church board members, I shared that I was very well-received at my current church and that I was not prepared to move if I just got the board's bare minimum vote (two-thirds). I told them I would need a vote of support of, at least, 80 percent to accept their offer.

(In addition to leaving a church where I was dearly loved, I would, once again, have to take a cut in pay). I preached that Sunday morning, and the superintendent preached Sunday evening. After the evening service, I left the room for the discussion and vote on my candidacy. When I was invited back in, the superintendent declared that, in all his years of ministry, this had not happened before; the vote was 100 percent in my favor! God was speaking loud and clear about what my next step should be. Little did I know what God was going to want of me in this place. But the vote was 100 percent, and sometimes, we NEED that kind of assurance from God. God is good!

I pastored at this new church for a couple of years. One day, one of the deacons came up to me and shared about a man he had met. He asked if this man could share his testimony at our next "Men's Ministry" meeting. I said sure, that would be great. He had been a schoolteacher for several years; then, he decided to quit and start his own landscaping business. He'd gotten saved and was so excited about what God had done for him that he wanted to share this good news. He wanted to be a "light" (Luke 8:16). He prayed every day, "Lord, please, use me." Then, his prayer became very specific. "Lord, please send seven people my way today, and I will share You with all seven." Every morning, that was his prayer, and all day he **looked** for those seven. Over the next year and a half, if I remember correctly, he personally led 187 people to Christ.

Wow! I was blown away by this testimony. I had been a Christian all my life. I had now pastored at a couple of churches, and I had given many altar calls where people gave their lives to Jesus.

But on a one-to-one basis, I had not come *close* to the number this new Christian had led to Christ. His "light" was shining brightly to unbelievers and believers alike, all for the glory of God!

4

My Nathan Assignment

I am about to discuss a matter that may distress some readers. It certainly distressed me at the time I confronted it. I feel it is important to write about it anyway, however, because I want to be careful to make sure anyone reading this book understands God sometimes orders our steps in ways that do not "feel good" in the moment. He may ask us to experience some suffering for His sake in order to accomplish His greater purposes. Like Job, we may be "perfect and upright" (Job 1:1) yet be called upon to suffer anyway. And God may or may not tell us what His purpose was in allowing us to suffer.

While I was senior pastor at this new church, the church district's officials held an annual business meeting. All ministers in the district were invited to attend. At this meeting, the district's financials were presented for approval. This particular year, the statements were extremely bleak. As a senior financial executive, I have come to realize that financial reports can tell very revealing stories. If you ask the right questions, you learn a great deal about what is going on "behind the scenes," so to speak.

In a preliminary meeting, I asked the district officials a few questions related to these financials. The questions asked exposed some troubling facts; however, the district officials did not appear to know what their answers revealed.

If I had stayed where I was and continued pastoring down south, I would *not* have been in a position to see or question the financials. The district superintendent, himself, declared the 100 percent vote that brought me to this district and the confrontation I call my "Nathan Assignment" (see 2 Samuel, chapters 11–12).

Nathan was a prophet of God and was told by God to confront King David, concerning his behavior related to Bathsheba and her husband, Uriah. He confronted David in such a way that King David pronounced judgement before he knew who the guilty party was. The judgement was hard, and then, Nathan declared him, King David, to be the guilty party.

David, you see, knew that adultery and murder are sins. He, however, had rationalized his own behavior to such an extent he no longer thought his actions counted as "adultery" or "murder." Satan deceives many, and many people simply deceive themselves while going along, feeding their sinful appetites. Christians, whether in a leadership role or not, do the same thing that King David did; they rationalize their behavior until they no longer think of it as sinful. James 4:17 (NIV) says, "If anyone, then, knows the good they ought to do and doesn't do it, it is sin for them." If, however, we practice self-deception and avoid accountability, who knows how long it will be before we no longer recognize sin as sin?

In the situation I am discussing, the district had foolishly gotten into the lending business and made some extremely bad loans to a non-church organization. Sadly, this non-church entity went bankrupt, and the loans became worthless. As a CPA, the failures of these officials in the handling of these transactions were obvious to me. However, it was not, at all, obvious to most of the other ministers.

I fasted and prayed about the situation for three days. I must admit this was the first time I had ever fasted for more than one day. I knew that my last "step" (ordered by God) had brought me, a minister and a CPA, to this point. I asked the superintendent for a meeting, and my request was granted. When I asked him what the district intended to tell the membership about their bad decisions and the resulting huge losses, I was shocked to hear him say it was "history," so "let's bury it." But nothing "buried" is hidden from God, as I remembered from Joshua 7.

Before the famous Battle of Jericho, Joshua told the people that **everything** (with the exception of certain items for the LORD's house) and every person (except for Rahab and her household) in Jericho must be completely destroyed. After the victory at Jericho, however, the Israelites were soundly defeated at Ai, a place where they'd anticipated an easy victory. When Joshua cried out to God and asked why, God said, "Israel has sinned and broken My covenant! They have stolen some of the things that I commanded must be set apart for Me. And they have not only stolen them *but have lied about it and hidden the things among their own belongings*" (Joshua 7:11).

Do you see how God emphasized the disobedience, the theft, and the lie? As it turned out, an Israelite named Achan had risked the *wrath of God raining down on him, his family, and his entire race, rather than repent for the theft in the first place.* If you take the time to read the rest of the story, it may shock you just how many steps Joshua had to take to get Achan to break down and confess the location of the stolen property. How far a man will go to avoid confession and consequence! We have such a loving God, who has promised to forgive us if we confess, yet time and time again, we refuse (1 John 1:9). WHY? Perhaps, we are not afraid of God so much as we are afraid to see that we have "feet of clay" just like every other child of God. Swallowing one's pride is, at least, one of the proverbial bitter pills, after all.

God is looking for **humble** and courageous servants. The Word tells us to humble ourselves in the sight of the Lord (James 4:10). If we refuse to humble ourselves, then, God will often see fit to allow humbling events into our lives, for our own good. Pride is better dealt with sooner rather than later, for it often hinders us from surrendering to God's will, and God's will for us is always far, far better than anything we can think up for ourselves. If it is not dealt with, however, we may refuse to take the steps GOD wants us to take and/ or refuse to do what is right in the eyes of the Lord. For Achan, his pride led him to believe that he "deserved" a little reward, and no one would know about it anyway! Ultimately, however, Achan, Joshua, and the entire nation received God's clear message; nothing we try to bury is hid from God, nothing!

Back to my discovery that I was to be the bearer of bad tidings when I least desired to be. I felt like Nathan in the Bible with a dangerous message to deliver. Instead of King David, my message was to the district leadership. These leaders needed to ask for forgiveness, for God's Word commands confession (James 5:16). They needed to confess in order to humble themselves before God and their fellow brothers and sisters in Christ. They had been extremely poor stewards of God's funds but had simply rationalized away their sin. Unlike King David, who repented, these men hardened their hearts and asked me, "Who do you think you are?" It is so, so sad when religious leaders cannot ask for forgiveness, when they are callous concerning their fellow man, and believe they are above fellow sinners. What they have become is modern-day Scribes and Pharisees. These very men preached repentance from the pulpit yet failed to follow their own advice. We have all heard it many, many times; actions speak louder than words. Their actions (and inaction) showed what they *really* believed, and it wasn't God's Word. Had they believed, they would have realized they had failed in their Biblical responsibility to invest their talents wisely and honestly give an accounting when asked. (See Matthew 25:14–30; Proverbs 13:11; and Proverbs 28:19.)

I knew that many people would be devastated if I brought the matter to the attention of non-Christian authorities. I also trusted that GOD is not mocked (Galatians 6:7) and that He would deal with the guilty parties in His own timing. My affiliation with that denomination was over, but the International Ministerial Fellowship (IMF) welcomed me in with open arms.

The story goes on and on with steps being made that in retrospect must have been "ordered by the Lord." God does this for all who TRUST HIM, WHO LEAN ON HIM, WHO, IN ALL THEIR WAYS, ACKNOWLEDGE HIM. For those children, HE WILL direct their PATH (Proverbs 3:6).

The Rocky Road

Unlike most ministers who have few options when they resign from a church, God had prepared me well for my next step. My journey to my ultimate destination, however, reminds me a little of Joseph's journey in the book of Genesis.

Joseph died in 1445 or 1444 BCE, but there are very few Christian, Jewish, or Muslim people who are unfamiliar with this son of Jacob. With no particular effort on his part, he became his father's favorite son. Favoritism generally inspires jealousy, and it certainly did in Joseph's family. It went beyond simple "jealousy," however. His brothers sold him into slavery and would have killed him outright if it wasn't for the "intercession" of one older brother by the name of Reuben. What followed may make some people think Reuben didn't do Joseph any favors.

To travel in a slave caravan from Canaan to Egypt over, shall we say, a long "rocky" road was unpleasant, by anyone's definition. Then, Joseph got a "break" working for Potiphar, captain of a palace guard, where he was sexually harassed and, then, falsely accused by Potiphar's wife. She wasn't satisfied until she got Joseph sent to prison.

The Bible shares very little of what Joseph actually thought about during his long trip to Egypt or his unfair imprisonment. Had he wrestled with anger and bitterness; he would have been only human. After all, the people who should have loved him committed crimes against him! I am quite certain that he did not whine about violations of his rights. After all, where would it have gotten him. Nor did he plot his revenge. God does not help someone who is harboring evil in his (or her) heart. Had Joseph remained bitter, it is not likely God could have continued to lead him and use him for God's greater purposes. For God is always true to His word, and His Word has this to say about bitterness and self-pity: "Let all bitterness and wrath and anger and clamor and slander be put away from you, along with all malice. Be kind to one another, tender-hearted, forgiving each other, just as God in Christ also has forgiven you" (Ephesians 4:31–32).

Joseph may have landed in jail, but while there, he befriended a couple of men who were being disciplined while on the pharaoh's staff. Because of those early steps Joseph took—i.e. to learn what he could, help others, and do the best that he could no matter the circumstances—Joseph became the second most powerful person in all of Egypt, and Jacob's family (Israel) was saved (Genesis 39). Joseph's job in Egypt was very different than the one he had working with his father, Jacob, tending sheep. The journey God has for us may take many turns, require us to climb some spiritual mountains, or simply stand still and wait. My journey may not look like yours; it certainly hasn't looked like Joseph's. The crucial thing is the *attitude* we embrace along the way.

5

A New Journey in Business

I found myself, once again, at a place where a major change in my journey led to very different steps in the business world. These steps were taken after my years as a full-time minister had come to an apparent end. Maybe, it will be a small demonstration to you of what these scriptures are saying to all of us and an encouragement for you and me to continue to "press toward the mark for the prize of the high calling of God in Christ Jesus" (Philippians 3:14). The purpose of this writing is to encourage you that no matter what comes your way, if you TRUST GOD, He is sufficient, and He will walk with you!

Wherever you are at, God is not only watching over you, but HE has a plan for you. He is NOT finished yet, so trust HIM with all your heart in the difficult time and stay focused on Him when you have mountaintop experiences. In some aspects, my life is not very different than almost everyone reading this. The names, places, and job titles are different, but we all face challenges, and we all need to daily place our trust in the Lord.

A businessman I'd worked with before needed some help upgrading his company's management and accounting systems. (This businessman, by the way, is the same person who served on that first church-building program committee with me several years earlier.) I worked with him for a few months, installing and tweaking the new system. I, then, created the financial reports the business needed. He was delighted and wrote the software company. The software company, over the next few years, referred me to over one hundred other businesses up and down the east coast, needing similar services. I now had a financial-consulting business. Taking one step resulted in the door opening for many more. It was a simple step to help a great friend. It turned out to be a successful journey helping one client after another and enabling me to take care of my family.

I did not have control over where I would be offered the next opportunity (but God did). At a few of these opportunities, I had the privilege of sharing a portion of the Good News. I trust you also share when God opens the doors and gives you the opportunity. (These are good steps for the kingdom of God!)

Steps of Learning

God had something new in store for me. Out of the blue, I received a call from a family member who lived down south. She worked for a businessman who had six or seven small businesses. The financial reporting had been done by his controller and accounting manager (husband and wife team).

As a responsible controller, he had purchased some new software. However, before he had a chance to install and transfer the data, he had a massive fatal heart attack right there in the office. His wife was not able to return to work—to the same office her dear husband had passed away in. This left the businessman with no one in accounting. It was late 1999, and the software was not 2000 compliant. This meant in a couple of months, their systems wouldn't work right.

I called the businessman and offered my services. I was immediately hired, sight unseen. No other time in my history was I hired this way. As it turned out, he was also a man who had pastored for several years. We bonded quickly. This time, the market was better, and I was able to sell my house quickly. I also found and purchased a house close to my new job. Although I was not familiar with either software package, handling new software was a common occurrence in my previous assignments. As a result, the conversion was done quickly and smoothly. Everyone in his organization was a Christian, so I thoroughly enjoyed this "step" in my journey with Jesus.

But It Was Time for Another Step

A businessman from my past called. Yes, that same man that served on the first church-building committee with me. A bank had offered to buy his business, and he asked if I wanted to assist him in integrating into the bank. I told him I appreciated the offer, but since the bank was acquiring the business, the bank CEO would need to authorize the hiring.

Typically, in banking, a banker is a banker, and normally, you rise up through the ranks. You don't come into a senior management position with zero banking experience. I had zero. The CEO, however, invited me in for an interview. His take was a little different. He said that they did not have anyone with a very diverse background like mine and offered me the job, on one condition; I would also do special projects for him. And that house that I had purchased less than a year earlier? God found us a buyer willing to offer sufficient funds to cover 100 percent of what we'd paid in buying the house.

This step, by the way, wasn't just for a job. God had brought us to a new church to plug into. I may have forgotten to mention it along the way, but with every move, God had us connecting with new bodies of believers. He always does; we just need to get planted. Planted means more than just going to Sunday-morning services. Even though I was getting older, I still loved playing in a church softball league. I convinced the pastor to let us start up a team. At the end of the season, we made it to the championship game against a church I used to be assistant pastor at. We lost the game, but it was a great success for Christian fellowship.

6

Hard Steps

My hard, hard steps are undoubtedly different than yours, but God allows these steps for His benefit. We like to call them the "fiery" times.

The bank I was working at was bought out by a bigger bank. My management position was redundant and, therefore, eliminated. I was unemployed, and God had not already given me a new job.

This time, I needed to wait, and wait, and wait and still keep trusting HIM. I got to spend hours, days, and months waiting and trusting. In these kinds of situations, waiting was a little harder, as you all may know, and trusting was a test of faith. Each of us would prefer to "sidestep" these, but God uses them to help "refine" us into the child that is pleasing to Him.

In the midst of this hard time, another hard step came my way. My wife met someone else. When confronted, she chose him. It is so, so common for us to say, ask, or even cry out, "God, where are you? Don't you see what is happening to me?" I am reminded of the poem *Footsteps In the Sand*. It is during these times He is carrying us, if we let Him. He is NOT gone; He is closer than ever. You just have to *trust* Him.

As a result, I needed to find a new job, sell the house, pick up the pieces, and press on. A lot of steps to take, but I knew I was not alone; God was with me. This did not stop the enemy from trying to convince me that I was alone. During this period, I applied for hundreds of jobs, all over the country. Many companies did not write me back, and others said they had other candidates. Some Christians have a very hard time with the rejections. I relied on God's Word where He declares that He opens doors no man can shut and shuts doors no man can open (Revelations 3:7). It is part of His ordering our steps.

I did not want to be alone, so what was I going to do? I went on a Christian website and found someone special on the west coast (I lived on the east coast). We got to do a lot of talking, getting to really know each other before we actually met. We fell in love, and shortly thereafter, she came east, and we got married.

7

Pressing On

I still wasn't employed, but I had a partner through these hard steps. Finally, I got invited in for an interview from a company that—the owner's son honestly admitted to me—was on the verge of bankruptcy. If I was willing to take the risk, I was hired. On the surface, this seemed to be a shaky step but a step, nevertheless.

This job brought me to a new community where we plugged in to a church with a choir that had over one hundred voices, led by an internationally renowned music minister—**Ted Cornell**, the music director for the Billy Graham crusades for many, many years. I felt like I was singing in a heavenly choir every Sunday! We also plugged in to a care group and into Stephen's Ministry. It just so happened our care group was blessed to have Timothy Seaman and his wife as part of the group. Timothy is an accomplished hammered performer with more than a dozen CDs. For one Valentine's Day gathering, Tim wrote a song for his wife. He asked if I would join him on my accordion. Subsequently, he asked if I would play this song with him on his next CD. I may not be a gifted accordion player, but this step allowed me to be a recording artist.

Even though, for the time being, God had turned my path away from full-time ministry, I knew I still needed to connect with other believers. In fact, every step we take, we should look for places to plug in. That is one reason why God directs our path in the first place. Link up and let your light shine! Speaking of linking, I would like to encourage everyone to join a church care group (small group). If your church doesn't have them, I encourage you to start them. It is great to get together with God's children; to share, to care, and to fellowship. The Word tells us to do it more as we see the day of His return coming (see Hebrews 10:25).

Back to work. A couple months after I arrived, a legislative change in Washington resulted in a huge increase in business coming our way. I am sure this legislative change was not a surprise for God, but it was good for us. In just three years, we went from five million dollars a year to over three hundred million dollars. I was reminded again of the seven years of plenty in Egypt, then seven lean years. Are we being good stewards in those years of plenty? The better the steward we are during the good years, the better we are prepared for those leaner times. Shortly after the sudden increase in demand for our services, I prepared a PowerPoint presentation for the owner and his son, demonstrating to them the significant increase in the value of the business and the narrowness of this opportunity. A few months later, they, in fact, sold the business capitalizing on this temporary increase. But as quickly as it came, it also went away. Just a few years later, the market stalled, and this company went out of business. Not only are the steps we take important, but sometimes, the timing is even MORE important. Isn't it good when we do things in God's timing? Had this businessman sold the company just one year earlier, he would have gotten millions less. Had he waited a year or two, he wouldn't have gotten anything at all.

West Coast and Back Again

The last step gave me experience in a specialized field, and that qualified me for a transition across the country, to Los Angeles. At first, it appeared to be a great opportunity; however, being in the same industry as my last employer, the "stall" they experienced significantly impacted my new company as well. As a result, my time here was shorter than I had planned. During the year that I was there, however, I did conduct some business with an entrepreneur that would impact a future step in my journey.

While in the area, we found a large church in Corona, California. WHAT A BLESSING! This church was not afraid of offending people by having "altar calls." In the year we lived there, at every service, there was an altar call, and people got saved—at every service! I felt like I was in heaven, tears ran down my face every Sunday, as I (along with the angels in heaven) witnessed sinners getting saved. **Luke 15:7** tells you that in the same way, there will be more rejoicing in **heaven over one sinner** who repents than over ninety-nine righteous persons who do not need to repent. Over seventeen hundred (1,700) people made a commitment to Christ that year. This only happened because week after week, the pastor was not inhibited to having an altar call.

We may need to ask pastors why they don't have altar calls anymore. They appear to be sidestepping instead of taking God's step. Their sermon isn't the most important thing; reaching the lost is first and then feeding the sheep, as Peter was called to do. The "altar call" may be just what a sinner needs to hear to take the step for Christ.

This reminds me of a situation I found myself in during my college days. Being plugged in to the big church, I arrived a little late for the Sunday-evening service. My plan was to slip in to the first vacant seat on the isle. But instead, I had to go all the way up to the front of the church. This was the seat God had reserved for me that night. A huge step was about to happen.

To my right was a visitor, the California brother of someone in our youth group. We had prayed for him in our previous youth-group meeting. We prayed for his salvation while here, visiting. I also knew his brother was sitting on the other side of him. And by the way, this visitor was going back to California the next morning.

We sang, the preacher preached, and the pastor asked if anyone wanted to accept Christ as their personal savior. I peeked and saw him raise his hand. Next, the pastor gave an altar call, but he didn't respond. I thought his brother would have jumped to bring him to the altar, but he didn't. What was he waiting for? This is what he asked us to pray for in our last youth-group meeting. I literally began to sweat. I had a quick conversation with God as to why the brother should be the one to encourage him to go forward. The Spirit continued to tug at MY heart. I meekly asked him if he would like to go to the altar. He said yes, so we went (but no brother). I had the opportunity to pray the Sinner's Prayer with him. No one would have been in that seat if I had not sat there. God put me right there to take a step to help someone else take the biggest step of their life. This happened more than forty years ago, but it still brings tears to my eyes to know God put me there.

This was a life-changing experience for him. He didn't know what to do next. But what he did do was cancel his flight back to California so he could learn a little about this new walk with Christ.

Three critical steps were needed: (1) the pastor needed to give the altar call, (2) I needed to invite the brother to the altar, and (3) of course, he needed to respond, "YES!" Such a little step for me meant he took the biggest step he could ever take. Have you been willing to obey when the Holy Spirit nudges you to take a little step that God can do big things with?

Steps of Faith and Patience

In 2009, the financial market took a nosedive which significantly impacted my job in California. I was asked to take a pay cut by the Asian owner of the company I worked for, and he would not let me take a look at all the books. A CFO such as I would normally have had access to all the information I'd requested. When I talked it over with my wife, she had what some would call a strong intuition that I should resign. (She views these "intuitions" as the Holy Spirit putting His hand on her shoulder to move her out of harm's way.) I didn't have another job lined up, but even with the pay cut, we would still have adequate income and medical benefits. The Holy Spirit continued to stir both my wife's and my heart. At the same time, things grew stranger at my office. As my wife and I prayed about it, I agreed that this was God's leading and resigned. Much later, when the FBI started investigating the company, I realized I quit working there just in time. In hindsight, I see that God's timing completely protected my integrity. We moved back to our house on the east coast which, for "some reason," had not sold during our time in California.

I began looking for a new job. That search took a lot longer than either my wife or I anticipated. During my *year* of unemployment, however, we had the privilege and joy of, once again, singing in my favorite choir. That did not pay the bills nor put food on the table, however, so we decided to use the time to do something we'd talked about doing for years—breeding mini schnauzers! Our tech-savvy daughter-in-law helped us set up a blog. My wife also found some part-time work. And like Joseph in Egypt, we had had another season of "plenty" to help us face the lean times.

It is amazing how God does little things for us at just the right time. We weren't sure our very young male mini schnauzer ("Doodah") would be up to the "task," but our female (Zippadee) got pregnant on the first try! The puppies were born, and to our surprise, Zippadee had eight puppies! A big litter. And they were ready for sale just when our funds were about depleted. We were able to use the proceeds to make the next mortgage payment. Isn't God good? The Bible tells us that God owns the cattle on a thousand hills. Sometimes, we wish He would deed some of that to us. It seems like it would be so much easier to live life when you have plenty; however, Israel's response again and again was to turn away from God during their times of plenty. Food for thought.

We will be rewarded in heaven for our walk of faith and trust in Him, *especially* during times of trial, sickness, or persecution. An old Hymn comes to mind: "Trust and obey, for there is no other way to be happy in Jesus, but to trust and obey." Another is "It Is Well with My Soul." The song writer was walking through some *very* difficult steps in his own life. His wife and child had died in a shipping accident. He got on a ship, and when he came to the spot of the accident, he wrote this precious song that I love so dearly! For me, when times get a little hard, I love to turn to the scriptures and some of the old hymns. Some of my favorite scriptures are songs in themselves like Psalms 61:1–3 which begins with, "Hear my cry, oh Lord, attend unto my prayer... When my heart is overwhelmed, lead me to the ROCK that is higher than I."

And God Has Another Step

I received a telephone call from a Christian businessman asking if I was still looking for a job. He did government contracts, and the government told him he needed his CFO to be a CPA, which God had orchestrated for me in some previous steps. Here, I had sent out hundreds of resumes without success, and at just the right time, God had someone call me with a job opportunity! It was another rare opportunity to work with several Christians. Sometimes, we all wish the "calls" would come sooner, but God knows best, especially what's best for helping us mature in Him. God is the Master Gardener, and He wants us to *grow*. That full year of waiting and trusting wasn't always easy, but God was always faithful, and this was a testimony to others, both Christians and the unsaved. **Isaiah 40 encouraged both my wife and I during this time, especially verses 29–31:** "He gives power to the weak and strength to the powerless. Even youths will become weak and tired, and young men will fall in exhaustion. But those who trust in the LORD will find new strength. They will soar high on wings like eagles; they will run and not grow weary, they will walk and not be faint."

We were involved in a care group while here and offered to put together a Revelation Bible study. We were able to enjoy sharing with others about the end times and the soon-coming of Jesus. It is especially good for us to be involved with fellow Christians during these last days, and Revelation has some exciting things for this world we live in.

A Skip and a Jump

Government contracts dwindled for my Virginia employer, and layoffs began. I was in need of another job. Where would my next step be? I shared my need with the businessman that had me come in to upgrade his agency management systems once upon a time. He came back to me a few days later and told me about a client of his that had a need for a chief financial officer. We talked, and I was hired. I was on my way back north. The job worked out great, and I was able to help them a lot. I set up some new policies, procedures, and systems to help normalize revenue forecasts and remove the fluctuations that they had been experiencing. I was actually greeted, one day, in the parking lot by the owner's wife. She rolled down her window to thank me for coming because those fluctuations had been keeping her husband up at night, but now, he was able to sleep. We also got the privilege to plug into another wonderful church. My wife started co-leading a women's Bible study, and I was accepted into the church choir. In addition, one of the members was a Gideon, and I was invited to join the team.

This job was close to where I grew up, so I was able to visit with family and old friends while there. This step didn't last for very long, however, as another door was opening.

I had met a businessman in California a few years back and talked to him about the idea he had for a startup business in the green-energy market. Out of the blue, he called my cell phone number, one which I had not changed in spite of several moves. He asked if I was interested in helping to take the company public. This appeared to be the opportunity of a lifetime which I could not pass up. Our lease was up for renewal, so the timing to move was great. My wife had friends in California to check out a rental house we had found on the Internet. They filmed it for us, we watched the video, and it looked like it met all our needs, so we signed the lease. We even had family nearby to help with packing up the trucks.

We were just about packed. We only needed to drive my wife's SUV onto the trailer. Outside my field of vision, my brother was standing in the wrong place at the wrong time. As I drove the SUV up onto the trailer, the trailer moved unexpectedly and sucked my brother under the trailer and SUV. The pressure was making it difficult for him to breathe. I quickly found the jack and was able to relieve some of the pressure, temporarily. We called 911 right away, and they arrived within a few minutes. They had a tool with them that was perfect for this situation, and my brother was out.

The Bible teaches us to stand and to stand firm. It is found in Ephesians 6, Galatians 5, 1 Corinthians 15, and in several other places. HOWEVER, we need to stand in the right place at the right time, spiritually. Physically, my brother was standing in the wrong place at the wrong time, but spiritually, his heart was right with God, and God was GOOD! He brought my brother through the ordeal, unscathed. The ambulance took him to the hospital, and about three hours later, my brother and I were ready to make the big jump from Boston to California.

Once I had settled into my new job in California, a young man in my office shared that he doubted the existence of God. We talked some, and I was able to lend him a Christian movie called *God's Not Dead*. He didn't stay long at the company and resigned before we could follow up on our discussion. It was a small step on my part, and I am encouraged, however, knowing I was faithful to take the steps God entrusted to me. Often He wants us to just plant and water; God gives the increase (1 Corinthians 3:7).

I had a new job and a new search for a church to join. My biggest disappointment was we could not find a church where the pastor gave altar calls. It was also hard to find a church with a choir in our area. I love choirs, as does my wife, and neither of us wanted to settle down in a church that didn't believe in the choir ministry. We both have sung in choirs and look forward to singing in the heavenly choir. In fact, every time I enter into a church service and the songs are sung, I feel like I am auditioning for God's heavenly choir. God, Himself, is listening to me sing and examining my heart as I sing. As I mentioned before, for God, it is not all about quality of the voice but the attitude of the heart. When you sing, do you sing to GOD, and is it from the bottom of your heart?

In traveling to and from work, my wife saw a billboard advertising a church. She took the step of researching it online, and *it had a choir ministry*. Very soon after our first visit there, a small group opened up. We quickly came to love each member and, in turn, they treated us with agape and respect. I was invited to lead a study I had drafted on the book of Revelation. The feedback I received from the group members encouraged my wife and I to flesh it out and finalize it. That experience opened us up to the possibilities of a writing career! How good it is to have rich Christian fellowship wherever

God puts you. I am so glad and so blessed that God has directed our paths to so many care groups along this journey. We have been encouraged and have been there to encourage others as well.

The journey has not ended, and I'm sure God has many more steps for me to take before I take that final step that lands me in heaven. What a GREAT step to look forward to. In the meantime, I need to follow my own advice; keep trusting the Lord, rather than trusting in my own understanding, and be a light wherever I stand. See Proverbs 3:5–6.

MAY GOD RICHLY BLESS YOU, and may you submit to His will as HE ORDERS *YOUR* STEPS.